# A Sense Of Self

Photos* And Writing By

## Kerri Lake

*except where otherwise noted

# DEDICATION

This is for You.

# ACKNOWLEDGMENTS

For all of the people who are stepping forward with courage to re-generate and re-define what it is to live on this planet, thank you. You inspire me.

Beyond the righting of any wrong, there are thousands of people now who have the courage to see things as they are so that change may truly happen. These pioneers are also seeing what has been and refusing to perpetuate what no longer works. These are the people who change the entire universe simply by being aware without judgment. The absence of judgment takes courage. It invites and creates change so fast that one day, most of humanity will just wake up, blink their eyes and wonder why anyone would ever have fired guns at each other in the first place. My friends, my team…thank you.

To those who are speaking and guiding humanity into a new paradigm, thank you.

To those who are willing to know they are right, then throw their rightness away to simply know the truth, thank you.

To those who have been treated without honor and recognize the opportunity to love rather than judge, thank you.

To those who are recognizing more opportunities to honor one another as aspects of the whole, thank you.

To all of the Beloved Ones who have guided, accompanied and assisted my own journey, thank you.

And a special thank you to Karen and Les Montgomery for their loving assistance in editing this book.

# CONTENTS

There are so many paths to enlightenment that have been taught throughout the eons of human existence, and there has always been the profound being of nature to guide us.

But with every path, with every teaching, there is a time when we are invited to step beyond our teachings, to step beyond the comfort of the systems that supported us and enter a whole new conversation.

Ultimately, the purpose of every system is to transcend it. You have the ability to go direct to your own source, and share it, as you wish.

# NO FRAME OF REFERENCE

Conflicts of all sorts collapse around me, and I can feel wide open space. More is moving now than ever before. Accelerated stages of integration become very evident through the physical form. That means the body is going to feel it! And the sensations are beyond description. The mind is totally at a loss with nothing to overcome. Now the conversation has moved into how not to create new conflict in this open space…

It is so unfamiliar!

It feels like being wide-open-vulnerable, a "sitting duck," so to speak, for whatever the universe has in store for me from whatever angle through whatever human instrument or beyond. The strangest part is not excluding humans from the "safe" list. Animals, easy. Trees, no worries. Humans too now get a reprieve from the defenses, free to be included as "Sources Of Universal Gifts".

Like I said, there have been some changes.

There are a million things to feel. Actually, more than that. It all feels very different. My part in the dance is "higher levels, let nothing but love come to me, let nothing but love be expressed through me and as my fullest expression..." It's getting easier since I am aware that this dynamic exists. I'm sharing with you so you can be aware, too.

With eons of training and pressure to not feel, to perform no matter what, to be what someone else might want to see, how could you expect yourself to have mastered feeling until you actually walk through it? Walking through it means not holding on to things that don't change. It means releasing the stranglehold on control. It means taking the mental levels, the mind's sense of safety to a place where it has no point of reference.

Change is a ripe environment to feel and sense beyond "the way it is, the way it always has been." So much flexibility is asked of the mind during times of change, and the mind wants to know what to expect. It wants to know so desperately that it will actually build several potential outcomes that may or may not have anything to do with what you're actually walking through, just so it has something to analyze! As long as the mind has a potential to analyze, it can determine itself to be "right" and therefore "safe." Great change leaves almost no clues pointing to an outcome that the mind may consider recognizable, and familiar is all it wants to see.

The mind goes looking when it has no frame of reference in new and unfamiliar territory. It goes looking through its annals of history, producing familiar images, stories and ideas that invoke familiar sensations. There is so much to feel, and the mind thinks it can control the whole show.

At least it wants to think that. A mind thinks the emotions and sensations should tuck neatly into commonly labeled categories in case an explanation or an escape should be required.

Feeling however, is not the mind's department. The mind can not feel. It can produce images and histories and suggestions that invoke chemical responses in the body. It can trigger all sorts of adrenal responses based on historical perspective, but it can not feel. The body feels. It is the body that senses.

In an environment of "no frame of reference," the mind has no control over what the body feels. You get to be there and watch it all happen! There is nothing to overcome - and this is a beautiful beginning.

Buzzing, prickles, tingles. Nausea, elation, dizziness, fuzziness. Ease, freedom, pressure, blah-ness. Light-headed ness … It cracks me up when people say they want to feel lighter, then their body goes a little dizzy with the changes.
The mind says, "Stop! There's something wrong!"

Let the senses happen. Let the mind know, "Mind, you are safe. This is sensational!" Watch how the body knows what to do without interference from mental controls. Watch clarity permeate the entire scene. There is nothing to do - you can sit still with your cup of coffee and enjoy feeling so alive. When the movement is allowed to move, it always keeps moving until the next open space makes itself clear.

It takes willingness and courage to watch your sensory experience in these ways, to watch and get to know Your unique common senses. Changes can move through like locusts. It takes courage to walk through the sensations of change and the conflicts generated by the mind just for the opportunity to know yourself in the absence of conflict. It takes love and the absence of judgment as you hold on to none of it and watch your innate clarity arise through every tone and frequency. Breathing helps.

It's a new paradigm full of how much life is here for you. I can't tell you how it's all going to happen for you - you get to feel it for yourself.

## PARADIGMS

Humanity has been operating from a state of rage for a very long time. Rage itself is a pretty big topic with a broad range of expression. There's the age-old hand-me-down rage that says, "This guy told me that god says I should hate you, so I do." And there's the less obvious, more insidious and self-destructive rage that survives a feeling of helplessness with the justification

that, "it must be my own fault somehow". It's taken a lot of energy to not only maintain the rage, but to carry on despite it. Most of humanity does not know how to function without it.

The old paradigm of untruths, low integrities, and other sneakinesses of historical leadership are being exposed for all to see. Watch the confusion of the masses bubble to the surface. Watch how things look messier before they look prettier. Would you call the changes "bad?" Would you call them "good?"

You will always have the option to hang on to the old familiar paradigm, but there is a new paradigm already created, forming and functioning alongside for you to step into. In a new paradigm, more people realize their freedom and use their awareness to create harmony. The rage dissolves and diffuses.

People who write, speak and share awarenesses of a new paradigm may appear confused at first in how they present their awareness. They may seem inconsistent. We are headed into uncharted territory. We may even need to make up some new words and concepts along the way. Even with the unfamiliarity, the heart has an innate capacity for gentleness in this new environment.

As you emerge into a new paradigm, the mind may still search for some form of conflict, something to complain about, because that is what the mind knows. Conflict is familiar to the minds of individuals as well as the collective "mind" of humanity.

In a new paradigm people find themselves hard-pressed to create judgment and conflict where none exists. Conflict proves to be unnecessary. And this IS new territory.

Listen with your heart. Let your own sense, that gentleness of heart, come into your awareness no matter what is being presented. You know the truth when you feel it. The truth is a vibration, a frequency that invites harmony.

As you acknowledge that nobody's mind actually knows the truth, you can begin to feel the vibration of truth uniquely through your body, a sensation that all can feel but is eternally unique to You.

## YOUR ABILITIES

I invite you to explore and expand your innate abilities as an aspect of Creator Consciousness, and to remember and communicate on sensory levels. Your connection with your own higher levels and with the other species who share our worlds is ever-present. You can let go of everything that has been made to be more important than who you are and fully embody your uniqueness throughout all of creation.

Your own higher levels of consciousness are the Presence, the guidance, the awareness of communion with all of life. Old teaching paradigms talk about seeking the divine. In a new paradigm you have the ability to instead call in your higher levels, integrate the consciousness and awareness and embody that lightness of being.

The Animal Kingdom, the Elemental Kingdoms, and Off-Planet support are with you in partnership as you step forward in this exponential evolution of consciousness. They are evolving right beside you, celebrating you with every courageous step you take.

Times of discomfort and confusion are your higher levels gently guiding you toward your natural state of ease and flourishment in life. Karma, suffering, earning and toiling are no longer necessary to realize new levels of awareness and communion. Your awareness can take you directly into communion with all of life, integrating your higher levels of consciousness with and as your physical presence.

You are a brilliant light on this planet, just as you have come here to be. With the support of all species and all forms of life, we welcome the greatest expression of you!

# WILLINGNESS

Watching other people open up. It's the most amazing gift.

You have the capacity to assist their flowering with simple recognition of their capacity to open their hearts. You don't need them to open up right then and there. Just know that they can, as they wish. Assist them when they ask. They will shift as they are willing.

To be willing to shift is a relaxation of the mental/egoic grip on control of what life should feel like. You can call it being afraid of the unknown, but it's not really a fear. It's a repetition of what's familiar, of what the mind has already experienced. Maintaining control of what's known will insure the control of what's familiar. Even when your heart knows that something unfamiliar exists and that's where you're headed, the mental/egoic filters can still avoid it and maintain control over your journey to the unknown.

The thing is, the unknown is often vilified before it's recognized. The mind can predict that the unknown must be something rash and uncontrollable. This is again the egoic/mental level doing what it knows how to do. It will create a fearful perception, reinforce that perception with sensations it knows how to control, and interpret itself to have done a good job surviving.

In this new paradigm of consciousness, you don't have to deny the old mental/egoic system to transcend it. You can let the mental/egoic levels plan their controls and call forth your expansion anyway.

Who You are does not stop when the ego exercises its muscles. You can watch the show, get a nice bowl of popcorn and let the sensations roll through the body. The most unfamiliar part is in refusing to fight it!

Who You are has nothing to prove, nothing to resist, nothing to offend, nothing to defend. Your golden essence emanates right from the center core of your dimensional being even while the egoic/mental levels are dancing dancing dancing around. Amazingly, your clarity is perpetually enhanced. You see yourself more clearly for the essence that You are.

You begin to happen.

## RELATIONSHIPS

Humanity spends so much energy protecting itself from relationships that are somehow "bad". It may not look like protection on the surface. It may look like success, or planning, or logic. It may look like principles, rules and standards. All very justifiable. And within all of that, relationships still exist. You have relationships with everything you judge to be "bad" or "good." To pretend otherwise is to live in denial.

Harmonic relationships do not include "good" and "bad." They make a priority of your own awareness rather than a perception of how a relationship should be. Life is more fluid when there is less conflict. And you know that trying to control things, especially other people, creates conflict, right? When you drop the way you were taught life should be and instead make your own awareness the number one priority, you become the absence of conflict. You become the movement happening in any relationship, be it personal, professional, or even relationships still dancing in judgments and opinions.

Harmonic relationships let business relationships flourish. They let the beloved of your heart present right before you. They let families evolve. They let matters throughout the entire outside world open up and resolve. They dissolve the necessity for protection.

Harmonic relationships are collaborations with the Universe for the fullest expression of Your Self and the whole.

# THE INNOCENCE OF LOVE

The innocence of love has been sexualized, genderized, as if Love itself requires a gender to become viable, or even seen.

Love has no gender. The love that emanates through your heart does not require a gender or even an object of focus. It moves through all that is, every dimension, every direction, and amplifies with your awareness of its presence.

The purposes of societal approval, maintenance of agreements and ceremonial acknowledgements have been tied to love for thousands of years, creating a perception that is actually the opposite of the truth. You don't need a marriage to prove your love - love is the marriage of the hearts beyond social agreements.

That the body has a gender is a statement that you were never meant to be alone. Transcending the paradigms of "opposites-attract", one gender does not require another of any gender to be complete. "You complete me" is simply a perspective of an old paradigm. It creates another journey back to awareness that you are already whole. The gender of a physicality is an amazing gift which allows you to express the love that you are through the physical realm, through a sexual expression, a touch or a simple gesture of kindness.

The innocence of love has no requirements. It has only everything to share through and beyond ceremony, approval and constructs. The innocence of love offers to complement Your unique expression of wholeness, completely expressed in harmony with your body's gender.

Sexuality is not to be denied - it is divinitized when you recognize that it is not a requirement of love, but simply an embodiment.

# CLEAR THE WAY

I've said to a few people, "There's nothing you can tell me that I can't find out without you. So, if you want to teach me something new, tell me about yourself. Then you'll be sharing things I don't know."

This was before Good Will Hunting came out, by the way, which has a scene with Robin Williams' character telling Will Hunting (Matt Damon's character) almost exactly that same thing. And actually, that I'm not the only one who sees it this way supports exactly what I'm talking about - wisdom is accessible to everyone. The question is, who's listening?

So I'll tell you something about myself. The wisdom that's here, you can find it in your own brilliance. But maybe you don't know this about me.

There has been so much fear built up around my heart, fear that disguises itself as strength, fear that blends in so well with "normalcy" that bringing it to light is like trying to squeeze cream out of milk with a hug. The irony is that it takes what seems to be a "normal" interaction to make the fear clear enough so I can see it. A "normal" event in this context is, for example, somebody being kind to me.

Here I am, writing about kindness all the time, sharing about it, sharing tools, etc, ways to invite humanity to be kinder to each other and themselves. They work, too! The tools work! And somewhere in my dance has always been this little person's psyche who found no kindness in the outside world and at that time happily took on the self-assigned mission of creating kindness on the planet. This mission included forsaking the social things young suburbanite humans are expected to do, like having friends and enjoying life. My priority throughout all of life, aside from brief stints of distraction, was to prove that kindness exists. And I had to do it alone because it seemed that nobody else would understand.

That's quite a job considering that the kind of proof needed for success will also require that other people are not just interested but also willing to see what I want them to see. But as a young person, maybe 3 years old, that logic had not yet formed itself.

Later, around age 14 it was more obvious to me that I had something to prove. At that point it seemed totally justifiable, in fact righteous to prove to someone, to anyone, that life is beautiful, simple, elegant. Totally full of love. Somehow though, I was still misunderstood by those closest to me. According to the people around me at the time, a young teenager growing up in Silicon Valley suburbia is not supposed to understand these things. A person my age was supposed to be defying parents, lying, struggling, chasing boys, preparing for the miseries of adulthood and fearing just about everything. That wasn't me, but it was hard to not be what they expected to see.

I spoke to them about how to feel the truth. I tried to share with my family how to heal wounds and injuries. I shared techniques for listening and interacting with animals, with guides, with consciousness, with the answers to any question you could possibly ask. I was told to tell the truth. I was told I was too sensitive. I was told that I couldn't see past the tip of my nose. Years later my father told me, "If I had known then what I know now, you would have been in an institution." I still celebrate his ignorance.

There was a point in there that shattered my confidence in my Self, confidence which was at the time very much synonymous with god. God was a feeling. A sensation. It was a sense of having at least 7 other presences guiding me, answering my questions and listening when I was confused or needed a way to prove to myself that I wasn't insane. There was a point where all that I had tried, all of the truth that came because I had declared my unavailability to anything BUT the truth crumbled all around me. All in one swoop, all of my effort was shattered because no matter what I did, my family would still not see kindness the way I wanted them to. I took it as a failure of my systems, of my self, of god, and I resigned myself to start over from the beginning. The reasoning was…I might have missed something.

The truth was, I hadn't missed a thing. I asked for the truth and I was provided with the truth. It just didn't match my expectation of how the truth should appear. Had I continued to speak the truth to my family, I would have been showing them kindness. I didn't understand that the truth and kindness did not require that other people play along. It did not mean my family would play along. At the time, I was holding the behaviors of my family to be the greatest proof of my rightness in kindness - my parents would step into love when I "got it right." That assumption simultaneously empowered the fear and devastation of NOT getting it right. Fear of not getting it right keeps another from being welcomed into my heart … according to the fear. And, if I have missed something, according to the fear, to the degree that the immediate family is not interested in joining me in kindness, then certainly it would be a dis-service to invite or let in any other person. According to the fear.

With all of this "proof", the fear began to feel normal. It seemed scientifically proven. Fear was normal to the degree of being invisible.

It's been consistent for a long time. For a long time there was no way to see the fear, nor could I see an opening to allow anyone in. Everything matched the environment of failure I felt in small childhood, which is to say that it was still my job to prove to the world that kindness exists. Certain people did eventually come along who I thought might break the spell, if only they would see things my way. Other people didn't see what I could see, which seemed like proof upon proof that my job has only just begun. Life was full of fear, and it was easy to live by its creed if I simply never try to open the door to let someone in.

More recently, with the support of the same god-party from when I was small, and a few others, I've been able to recognize opportunities to connect with others. Beyond that, I've begun to open up and actually let them in!

Sounds great, right? Well, it's funny how much fear I still feel. It's funny how saying hello to someone and letting them return your hello with an openness and sincerity can feel threatening. It's funny how I can share with someone, remain aware of my own defenses and still refuse to use them. It's funny how easy it would seem to just "teach" something about kindness or consciousness. It's funny how raw it feels to feel openness from another and have no protection. It's funny how the sense of welcoming gets twisted and the defenses try to function in the face of openness.

Letting others into my heart is the untwisting of twine that looks like it's going to be a crazy mess just up until the point that the central aperture reveals itself and draws forth a sense of wholeness like a snapshot of that moment when everything can change.

What I'll share with you about me is that I still feel so much fear - fear of you showing up to be kind to me, to share support. I feel the fear, and I'm happy you're here. I can feel it. At least now I know it's there and we can address it. There is so much to share, and I can say that now not from having to prove to you what I see, but from having let myself into my own heart to clear away the righteousness and its parallel insecurities.

I wonder what it will be like to let more into my heart. I wonder what more will come for me to share.

# CLARITY

When you start to really go with your senses, to really run with what your Higher Levels are presenting, it takes you into a whole different essence of who You are.

I'm not talking about trusting what you are getting. It's not about trusting your intuition, or trusting the Universe. It's not about trust.

Trust turns out to be a head game where the mind is giving itself a little bit of leeway to present satisfactory and comfortable new data and information to make an informed decision within reasonable controls, producing new provable evidence of having been right or wrong to trust in the first place. … no, no, no.

I am talking about asking for clarity, being handed clarity, and running with it.

Clarity can feel like a place where there is no evidence for any particular outcome, no evidence that anything will ever be the same again or different. It can feel like having no evidence, period.

When you know you are running with your clarity, make this clarity the priority and watch everything keep moving forward. And still keep running with it.

Clarity is not about intention. Clarity requires no choosing. Those are both head games as well. You can ask for guidance and direction, be handed guidance and direction, and run with it.

Evidence can only prove what has not worked for you previously, so why search for evidence if what you're asking for is beyond all that you've ever known?

Ask and run with the lightest of hearts, knowing that a mistake is impossible and no matter what presents on your journey, you are doomed to success.

# PATTERNS OF SURVIVAL

The paradigm of "survival of the fittest", which was a great motivator at one point, is no longer effective for the direction Humanity is moving. We've passed a threshold. The energy of survival no longer has purchase. We are all fit to live, and if we choose to survive, then that is all we will do.

A new paradigm of life offers support in-between the thought structures and patterns we have been using to get by, the thought patterns that kept us in a familiar rhythm of survival. Can you feel it? Can you feel the difference? If you're not feeling it yet, if you are still feeling the pull of responsibility and competition, then imagine...

Imagine that there is space in-between the thoughts.

Imagine what it feels like to notice that someone has opened the door to the cage. You're still inside, but the door is open. You can see the bars that have held you in. Before, all you could see was the outside, never really bringing into focus the actual construct of the cage.

With the door open, the cage comes into focus. Is the cage significant? Do we have to study how the bars were constructed? What they're made of or how strong they are? Do we need to examine how long it's taken to get past them?

NO! The door is open! Fly! Fly through the door! You don't have to fly far at first … maybe fly out and sit on top of the cage for a moment. Get your bearings. Feel the world with the cage supporting you rather than restricting you.

Let yourself expand now. Watch. There is nothing to do. The expansion has been waiting for this moment, and it is here.

You expand out, out, into and through the world. You are received.

Sit on top of the cage until you're ready. Until you know that you know what direction to fly. And just fly!

You don't know what you'll find when you get somewhere, and even if you did, by the time you arrive...it will be different.

Feel the direction, and fly!

## EMBRACING THE SOURCE

So many facilitators, teachers, healers etc are masters at their crafts. They have done all of the studying, the courses and the achievements. They can talk just about anyone through what they know, and they have an unshakable confidence in their ability to be a practitioner of their modality.

And then the conversation goes to the places where there is this extra knowing that their modality doesn't quite cover. It's a knowing they've always had but haven't found a way to touch on because it just doesn't seem to be taught anywhere. Nobody seems to know how to talk about it. They have come to a place of acceptance about the whole thing. They'll call it a trust but it feels more like a resignation to sitting quietly in the chair with hands folded until the Universe delivers the next piece of the puzzle. For some reason, the structure of the teachings didn't include this part. So they wait patiently for the next sign.

This pause is the invitation to step beyond the system.

The purpose of each system is, ultimately, to transcend it. You are not a system. You are not an -ism or an -ology. You are a dynamic expression of Creator Consciousness. The systems are amazing tools to assist the mind to continue in a direction. The greatest perpetual expansion is in your uniqueness, beyond the scope of any system. The systems can point the way - the question is, will you actually go there?

When the answer is "Yes, I'll go!" without compromise, without a Plan B (or a Plan A for that matter), your higher levels share guidance, nudges and awareness through sensations that are undeniable, but not always comfortable. The guidance may seem odd. The guidance may seem to go directly against what has been taught by the systems that at one point represented a path to wholeness.

How can this be? The mental level might ask. How can it be that now, all of a sudden, my guidance tells me to do anything other than all that I've adopted as "the way?" Yet, somehow, the "going against" at this point may feel more true to your uniqueness than following the teachings or systems.

Embracing the guidance directly from your own source is never about denying what has brought you to where you are. It is the open invitation to explore more than the systems know how to manage. It is the invitation to recognize and embrace that You are a facet of the source that created those systems, and you can generate interactions with the out-ward world from that same source of Creation. Who you are is already beyond the structures that brought you to where you are.

Teachers, healers and facilitators have been taught that they require a big tool box, or the capacity to master specific tools in order to be potent in their craft. Now more than ever, it is your Presence that gets it done. Your Presences emanates the mastery of Love. The structures and modalities are and will always be the brilliant tools that they are. If power and potency are still important, the potency of tools will increase to the point of total integration as you continue to claim and embody all that You are - the Presence that the systems and tools were guiding you toward all along. Your Presence has been the generative source for the potency of the tools all along.

Who am I without the systems that carried me here?

## A CHANGE IN VALUE

The language we use now is designed from a perspective of well-defined linearity. There is a difference between correctness and incorrectness. Understanding has been geared toward the interactions of space and time, cause and effect, rather than a fluid expression of harmonic dimensionality. The physical world of rights and wrongs is just one dimension. Your senses make evident countless dimensions accessible through your awareness.

As You continue to step into "show me more of who I am" it's like watching layers of clear plastic wrap peel off, each one revealing more of your freedom from a predictability that was limited by an old-paradigm perception of "how things work." Now things can work without having to satisfy what used to be required "proof." The proof now is that you perceive it.

And then, "Show me more..." Step into it! The perceived lapse of time between asking and receiving reduces infinitely until it appears to invert. You come to a state where you recognize a creation before the awareness that it was even possible. This is You in total engagement with a creation and AS an integral part of the creation while it is happening.

All of humanity continues to move toward embodying their own unique higher levels of awareness and consciousness. Along the journey, the priorities for what we are collectively "looking for" begin to change and converge. Of course there will still be great diversity, great uniqueness, and even differences in approach. But there will also be greater and greater convergence for what is considered foundational to the awareness of all human beings. There will be a convergence toward a new understanding of "common sense." Humanity is converging into, and as, Love.

An economic system was never designed to serve humanity. Not truly. It was designed to serve itself, requiring humanity to conform for success. An economically-based system of valuation keeps people operating repetitively from an egoic level of consciousness. Shifting judgments of value equate with shifting emotional/egoic perceptions of need.

As humanity evolves and technology continues to become an integral part of how we express ourselves, remembering what it feels like to be unique and to express yourself uniquely is the real value of any one person's contribution. Even with so many tools available for communication, your uniqueness is still visible, sense-able in a world without barriers.

You become an opportunity for others to receive and respond to you with genuine kindness when you are authentic and undefended in how you say what you say. Trying to force someone to communicate with kindness doesn't work, but when you yourself are a presence of clarity, you then become the invitation to others to meet you there. Encouraging humans to feel kindness in themselves expands the greater capacity for kindness to all species and other forms of life as well. Relationships can flow with ease.

When priority and value are recognized as being inherent to one's presence and contribution, the functionality of an economic system will transform itself to a state where there is no lack.

Historically the system says "You are valuable if you can perform like this..." Higher frequencies of consciousness transform the paradigm to say, "You are valuable. Here is what is required. Thank you for your contribution."

You have the innate nature of kindness. You have the capacity. Now there are new tools. Will you show kindness?

## EXPONENTIALLY MORE

How can I express the extent to which you owe me nothing?
There is nothing I need from you
I lack nothing without you
And yet
Somehow
With you
I am
Exponentially more

## LOVE CLARIFIED

So often, Love is confused for understanding, recognition and approval. The confusion is all about safety. If there is familiarity and a certain level of comfort, it is safe to love, right? If there is understanding, empathy and compassion, that's love, right?

Beloveds, these things are wonderful. But they are neither requirements nor aspects of love, except in the sense that love is *all that is*. Understanding, recognition and approval are all constructs of the mental levels, aspects of safety. Of course the mind is interested in these things as tools for its own self-awareness and survival. But to see them for what they are is to recognize that they are constructs.

Who you are is so far beyond these things, requiring nothing of them, transcending them, being a Presence right through them to emanate your unique expression of All That Is.

Why would *All That Is* need to be safe from itself?

# INTEGRATION

The integration of all that you are is not a remedy for something broken.

It is an honoring of how far you have come, that you are still here, and that you are awakening to what is accessible to you. The simple awareness that you are awakening is enough. From there, how much can you enjoy the ride?

Your timing is YOUR timing. There is not a single other One on the planet who is where you are at this point along your journey. In this context, the concept of competition is beyond obsolete. You are the unique aspect of Divinity that you came here to be, and now you are supported more than ever, just say the word, and your Higher Levels, the angelic realms, the ascended host realms make themselves known right there by your side, assisting and guiding you to know so much more of all that you are. Watch as the world around you re-shapes its expression to complement and honor you.

The journey takes courage.

It takes you being willing to be loved. Really, how could you not be loved when you ARE love? But the assumptions required to survive the dense structures of an old paradigm built on judgments created a very real environment of the absence of You, the absence of love.

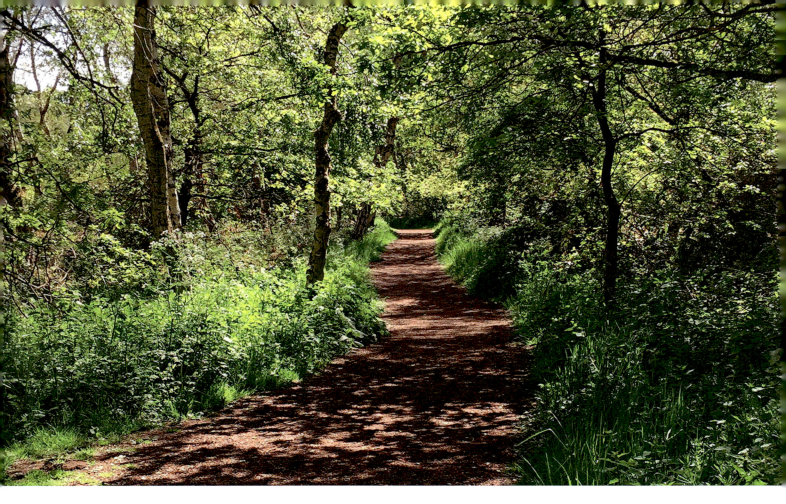

That is all over now.

You are coming forth into You, literally, like never before. You are unique, and you are an aspect of the whole. Without your presence in consciousness, it would all come apart.

There is no absence of You in all that is. The magnetic adherence to any thought of an absence of you is losing its strength and taking much more effort to maintain - this effort is the struggle you see when Dear Ones try to hold onto the familiar.

The love that you are is the space in-between all of those old, obsolete structures that will still function if you need them but truly no longer serve - structures that are absent of You, absent of your unique creativeness throughout all that is. The love that is You is the source of buoyancy already in place as the old structures dissolve.

Integration is a surrender to all that You are. To who you are. It is a surrender to your own access in the presence of love that is already in place as You open to let it into the spaces between the structures. You don't have to launch yourself out into nothingness - the love of Creator Consciousness, your Higher Levels, would never leave you without support. Integration is letting your Higher Levels in, surrendering to the wisdom and creation of You from those levels, and watching creation unfold from those frequencies and vibrations. The angelic, arch angelic, ascended host realm frequencies of You begin to dissolve that which no longer serves You and regenerate your physicality and entire world. You begin to emanate and honor all that You are. Integration acknowledges the Higher Levels of You by saying, "Come on in! I'm totally game! Show me what this is all about and show me how awesome this can be!"

Your welcomeness is a simultaneous intensity and gentleness, unmistakable as the Presence of Love. And that's You!

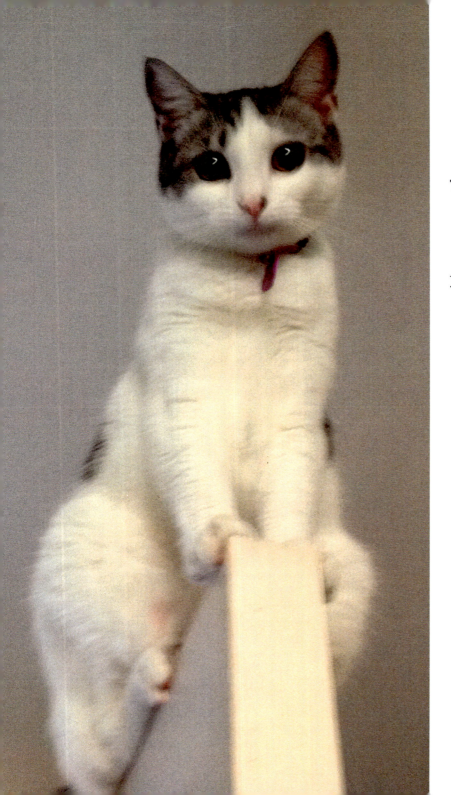

UNLIMITED

There are no limitations to You.

The physical world is limited by the nature of its construction. That does not mean that the physical world is a limitation to you. It is simply a system to be understood with clarity and used without judgment.

Ultimately, the purpose of every system is to assist you to transcend its limitations. The system has limitations. The physical world has limitations.

You are unlimited.

# NO WAITING

Every single person in your life, and on the whole planet for that matter, is totally in support and in LOVE with You running forth to drop the pretense, to show up and to nourish the brilliance that you are.

They may not recognize that brilliance when they see it. They may even use all of their resources to try and shut it down. It's just that they've never experienced life in this light before and they don't yet see their opportunity to dance in that light.

Keep going whether they understand or don't! The heart will recognize what it sees, in this life or the next. Every One has the capacity to step into what their heart knows.

Waiting around for another's awakening is just short of a hunger strike.

# NEVER ALONE

Here's the thing … Everything's going to be okay.

You are restoring your Self simply by acknowledging the changes you see around you, the changes you see within you, the changes you recognize AS you. See it without judging it and you Divinitize it.

Embodying your uniqueness, your divine essence is why you came here. It's who you are - the gift of your Presence.

We've been calling these changes "healing", but really it's regeneration. Regeneration is re-claiming all that you truly are, the unique vibration in all of consciousness that is You! As the changes move through you in very tangible waves - cold waves, heat waves, dry waves, electrical waves, history waves, love waves - let's honor that the mental levels want to be safe…

All is well. Of course the physicality will feel the movement. Mental levels might worry, but you are not alone. Watch the movement. Let courage assist you to see the truth without judgment. Relax the grip and watch the body feel the movement. It's just movement. It feels different, and different is exactly what's been called forth. Waves of nw movement will feel different to the body. You are not alone.

Higher Levels, all of Me, take command of the movement for my fullest expression, to complement who I am, intensely, gently, right where I am in my lifestream right here.

...I refuse to go through this alone.

# INFORMATION

Most people truly don't realize how much information is accessible in every direction at every breath just by asking.

Why do you suppose people are taught to learn in a linear order? Why do you suppose people are taught that they must be taught to learn before they're worthy to learn? It's commonly taught that you shouldn't know what you haven't been taught.

There is less about how to sense relationships in information rather than formulae for repetition of what seems important at the time.

It's valuable to see why information is valuable, perhaps even more than an ability to recite the value of it. There are endless ways to think about information, so why try to memorize them all? You can sense and see information and listen to it without understanding the full extent of its applications. When you have a familiarity with the value of an information, its applications will

make themselves obvious. Would you like to memorize all of the combinations of applications and values? Or would you instead like to be accessible to the opportunities to apply value? The memorization now, more than ever, is accessible in the collective knowledge through the internet. It's not your job to be the authority anymore. Your job is, should you choose to engage it, to listen and be willing to use your capacity to move or apply knowledge as the opportunities present.

Sometimes that will mean sharing straight-up information. Other times it will mean sharing sources. Still other times, you will share knowledge by opening the way for others to see that knowledge exists. And like the wise old man who rather than cooking his hungry neighbors a meal will instead teach them to fish, sometimes your part will be to guide others to know for themselves.

You are a fountain of value.

There is no measure to the value you have to share. Like, there is no scale that will measure the value, although you're taught to seek or create one. The value of sharing your value happens outside of a paradigm that requires quantification on paper or computer screens. The paper and computer values are just tools of analysis and awareness. They are tools that help us enjoy the physical world in increasingly diverse and creative ways. But they are not value. We're redefining value here... You are value. Will you give us the opportunity to recognize your value?

Will your family say that who you are is of value? Will they say you are the same value you say you are? How about the grocery clerks? Or your dentist…? Do you require their consensus to share your value? Do you require their approval, or even their recognition?

The questions are an invitation for you to know who you are. Where you stand. What you stand for. Whose value is running you? The more you let these questions guide your awareness, you will continuously uncover more of the value that you are and continuously see the endlessness of its generative source. Endless. Inexhaustible. It's another way to talk about divinity…but let's not get hung up on the language.

Follow the generative source and watch as the evolution of value becomes obvious. It's not that an evolution is "better", it's that a new definition already exists when you're willing to ask. Why not get with the times, eh?

I saw a great little image recently on Facebook, and it came with some words. It said, "This is a friendly universe. Don't believe me…test it."

I triple-dog dare you!

# HIGHER FREQUENCIES OF YOU

All of the density that seems so compelling, the "what about this and what about that and how do I change this or that or them", breaks apart in the presence of You as you let yourself arise and embody.

Higher frequencies of the light body create space in-between the particles of density, thought, and whatever was taught is required to work and work and maintain and maintain. The sensation is called "unfamiliar" as more space opens up to let You come through. This space is opening as a gift to you from your higher levels, inviting you to see that all is well, that there IS a You that is happening in-between and all around these particles of density that seem so magnetically obvious. There is nothing to fight - pretty unfamiliar - nothing to wrestle, nothing to change as it is all changing for you, around you and through you. Now, your part is to watch

it happen. Watch the space open up and see the particles for what they are - old thought forms, systems, beliefs, needs, misunderstandings, old structures that at one time served to hold you up like a scaffold and keep you moving through a world that enforced the opposite of ease.

The particles of density that fly around as they break up have nothing to do with you. Familiarity might be a compelling reason to re-identify with them, to grab on or let them stick as if you have something to do about it. Even if you grab back on to the familiar conflicts, you will begin to notice how much they just no longer fit for you, work for you, or even seem like a good idea anymore.

Now is different. Now you can see the particles for what they are. You can move throughout the space in-between them, letting them fly all around, perhaps even noticing their magnetic charge as they fly close by. But You are moving in and as the space in-between them, amplifying far more, far faster than the slow dense frequency of the structures. As your awareness expands, the light pours in. Higher frequencies of You move and expand the space between the particles of density so you can begin to see more clearly that you are You and density is density.

When you walk through a physical doorway, you don't approach the supporting structures, grab on to them and start working to reverse-engineer them, then question how they could possibly still be there and lament over their existence. You look for the space in between the structures and just walk through.

## YOU MATTER

Honor every One. Honor every thing, just exactly as it is. Exactly as it presents to you as you walk through every journey.

Let it be what it is without getting in a fight. As unfamiliar as that might feel, when you honor it all for what it is, the people and things that are of love and integrity will arise to the surface. The people and things, ideas and concepts that are absent of love or lacking integrity will also make themselves very clear. The point here is that it's not your job to figure out which is which. When you honor all things, all things come to clarity.

Honoring seems to be kind of a new concept. The mind wants to know if honoring a person or thing means you believe in it. Or is honoring that you think it's true? Or you agree? The mind might think that honoring means respect or some sort of a new-age "buy-in". The mind wants to know if honoring something or someone means giving up or sacrificing in some way.

Actually, honoring is more about the courage and openness to see the motivations behind all that presents and having no conflict with them. It's the willingness to see the truth and not judge it. It's the willingness to acknowledge when something or someone is complementary to my own life stream or otherwise, and it's the integratedness to let myself be complemented.

Honoring another person includes no sacrifice. How does it honor you if I am denying myself?

I'm walking through a market and a seller calls to me. He tells me he has the best apples in the market and his price is the best. I love apples - maybe he can see that. I turn and look at his apples. They are nice apples, and even so, my stomach gets tight. His voice has a soothing tone, but the sense of the situation leaves my body in tension. I am not interested in creating anything from that space of tension, so I address him, "Thank you for the offer!" …and I walk away. There are other sources of apples.

Some people use anger as a means to not deny one's self, and that's okay. Anger is a great way to break energy with another. It may be exactly how you feel, but it's still not a full honoring of one's self.

Some may confuse honoring with "love yourself." You already are love. Honoring is about acknowledging that love and engaging the world from that integrated knowledge.

The essence of honoring comes from an inexhaustible source - your divine heart-center. Your creator essence. Honoring says, "Yep, that happened. Yep, that's happening. And this is who I truly am. This is how I walk through a situation or relationship from my heart. This is how open I am to being loved, to being love."

Right about now the mind may start demanding the how-to's, right? How do I do that? How do I honor someone who's all up in my face? How do I honor someone who hurt me and then went away? How do I honor people who hurt others? How do I...? What if...? Yeah, but...? Those are all valid questions, and I honor them.

The big question is, what really works for You? And will you stop holding on to what doesn't work for you? With these questions you have engaged in a beautiful beginning to honoring yourself. You have transcended any righteousness for how the outside world should change to accommodate you. You are asking for clarity about your own flourishment and opening up to what that clarity will bring you. You are communicating to the whole universe entirely that you are willing and accessible to be loved. You are taking the first steps beyond a paradigm of judgment. You are reclaiming You.

Reclaiming You is the greatest honor you have to share with the world. Nothing needs to change - a new paradigm is not about forcing changes upon the outside world. You are creating the greatest changes by no longer denying the truth that You are. Being the truth that You are has no offense and no defense. You require nothing of the outside world except for it to be exactly as it is. You require nothing of yourself except to be exactly as you are. You listen, watch and sense for clarity in the direction that You are going rather than a old-world perpetual scan to avoid an imminent attack. You are dropping the weight and regenerating.

Many people who are newer to the planet already understand that historical conflicts once considered normal are actually extraneous. The argument that says "because that's how we've always done it" isn't getting it done anymore. There are so many here now who know where we are going, whether they would speak of it that way or not. They're everywhere. Authenticity matters. Heart matters. Uniqueness matters.

You matter.

# ABOUT THE AUTHOR

*Photo by Julie Fogg Vaccari*

Throughout my life, I have been aware of various levels of communication accessible to people. My parents didn't quite understand what was going on. After about 4 years of life, I was told that I can't possibly remember things that happened before I was born, the dog was not talking to me and the trees were definitely NOT telling me jokes. That was confusing because I was also told to tell the truth, which I had...and so an internal paradox began.

Being "good with animals" put me on a path toward veterinary school and eventually studying at UC Davis. Once I got there, though, it became immediately obvious that academia was not readily receptive of my gifts and way of being. I wasn't particularly fond of their ways, either. Even so, I finished my degree in Animal Science over a span of time while trying to find the courage and space to express myself in the ways that are totally natural to me.

I didn't have the vocabulary to describe it. I had no experience with other people who had the capacity to hear me. What I did know is that I was able to change the energy, space and consciousness in a room, a body, a barn, kennel, city, time frame, history...through a very simple and elegant sensory connection, through my presence.

Everyone is already equipped for their connection, but not everyone is aware of it, and most are taught to fear it. I only learned of modalities like Theta Healing, Reconnective Healing, Quantum Touch, etc, years after I had condemned myself as crazy and spent almost every last bit of my life force trying to be much less than I am. I was afraid to be different, I was afraid to be the same. I would play silently, everywhere, in "healing work" that has been described as

79

"healing with my being". I see everyone as whole. I see your entire being, and I can't find anything more awesome than you claiming the space to show up as all that you are! And finally I stepped into receiving the love and assistance that would facilitate my own emergence.

Divinity is all about your Presence. There is a whole world out there that's called "New Agey", and there is so much judgment around it. But my question is, what could be more foundationally pragmatic than clarity, understanding, and the courage to be honest with ourselves? That's what it takes to remember and bring forth your Uniqueness and divine expression.

The greatest gift I can offer you is the fullest expression of my own uniqueness without judgment. That space, the absence of judgment, is the magic, catalytic healing space that the natural and etheric worlds are for us. I know we can be that for each other in this new paradigm of arising consciousness, in our bodies as humans.

And what a beautiful world this is.

# INDEX OF PHOTOS

p57. The bridle path in Sherwood Forest, the actual Sherwood Forest in Nottinghamshire, UK, 2015

p59. My friend Hoku demonstrating the limitations of the physical realm - she would prefer to be higher than the top of the door. Haena, Kauai, 2014

p61. The view from seat 30A, somewhere over California, 2015

p63. The sky on the day I ate cake at Wadswick Country Store Cafe in Somerset, UK, 2015

p64. Volcanic mineral deposits near Lake Taupo, New Zealand, 2015

p65. An amazing sunset in Yachats, Oregon, 2015

p67. Faery tingles in the forest outside North Brewham, Somerset County, UK, 2015

p69. Overlooking Holyhead Lighthouse, South Stack, Holy Island, Wales, 2015

p71. Melbourne Botanical Gardens, Australia, 2015

p73. Cape Perpetua, Oregon Coast, 2015

p76. The herd at Wild Tender Ranch, Pescadero, CA, 2012

p79. Kerri after a springtime sledding day with a good friend at about 8000 ft, Mt Charleston, Las Vegas. Photo by Julie Fogg Vaccari, 2011

p80. A golden selfie!

Made in United States
North Haven, CT
12 October 2021